Stock Market Investment

Made Easy

Harold Watt

AuthorHouse™ LLC
1663 Liberty Drive
Bloomington, IN 47403
www.authorhouse.com
Phone: 1-800-839-8640

Published by AuthorHouse: 11/04/2013

ISBN: 978-1-4918-2825-0 (sc)
978-1-4918-2826-7 (e)

Library of Congress Control Number: 2013919433

This book is printed on acid-free paper.

authorHOUSE®

Understanding
The
Basics of the

Stock Market

DISCLAIMER

This book and all materials are designed to provide the reader with a basic understanding of the stock market. It is for educational and information purposes only. All stock trading involves risk. All decisions made to buy a stock are personal, and should be made after thorough research. The company's products, training, and coaching are for training purposes only. The company does not offer legal advice, accounting, or any other professional opinions. We do not solicit or recommend that you buy or sell any stock. If legal advice or any other expert assistance is needed, you should seek the services of a competent professional. This company is not liable in any way or form. You should consult a licensed broker or a registered investment advisor before buying any stock.

Introduction

   This book was written to help those who have an interest in playing stock market become more knowledgeable. It presents basic concepts to help you better understand the stock market and how it works. Although the stock market can appear very complex at first glance, anyone can do well in the market when taught how. In this book you will learn how to play the market which should eliminate any fear that prevents most people from ever trying. You will learn about fundamental and technical analysis, when to buy a stock and when to sell, the importance of market direction (uptrend, downtrend or correction), support and resistance, moving averages and stop losses. At the end of this book you should have the confidence to get started. You should also know how to increase your chances of success with the knowledge that you will attain while reducing your risk. I hope that you will continue to expand your knowledge in the world of investing. I would also like to wish you great success.

Table of Contents

What is a Stock Certificate?

A **stock certificate** (aka—*certificate of stock* or *share certificate*) is a legal document that certifies ownership of a specific number of shares of stock within a corporation. In large corporations, buying shares will not always lead to a stock certificate (this usually occurs when a small number of shares are purchased by an individual).

Here in the United States, companies are no longer required to issue paper stock certificates. In fact more than 400 of the many publicly traded companies do not issue stock certificates. All transactions or trading (buying and selling) is done through an on-line broker or brokerage firm. There are several brokers to choose from but the easiest way is to set up an account with one of the on-line brokers. We will discuss brokers in a later chapter. The goal here is to give a better understanding of what a stock or stock certificate is.

Market Psychology

Psychology (is defined as the mental behavior of an individual or group) plays a major role in the market. It can change the market's direction (at any given time) in a matter of minutes. There are two psychological factors that rule the market, Fear and Greed. The stock market feeds off of these two emotions. **Greed** is an emotion that can cost you dearly (if you are not careful) when playing the stock market. There are countless investors who have lost fortunes because they allowed greed to take over. A good investor knows when to take his/her profits (or lock in their profits). I will show you how (stop losses) in a later chapter.

Fear; Fear is an emotion that can paralyze you and prevent you from taking action. It can also be defined as **False Evidence Appearing Real**. Fear can and will set in after a loss or a change in the market's direction. There will be times when you have done everything right and the market changes direction on you. When this happens (and it will happen) you cannot let fear set in. You minimize your losses and you wait for the next opportunity. Once you learn how to analyze the market (as well as your stock) you will know when to get in and when to sit on the side line. We are all subject to greed and fear but learning to control our emotions will lead to great success when playing the stock market.

Fundamentals Analysis

What is fundamental analysis? Fundamental analysis involves analyzing the financial statements or health of a business. It involves looking at the management and any competitive advantages that a company might have (such as new products or services). Examples of a company's fundamentals (terms you should know) would be but not limited to, earnings per share, relative strength, sales and profit margin, return on equity, current earnings, annual earnings,

Earnings per share (EPS) is the amount of earnings for each outstanding share of a company's stock. In essence you want to see at least a 20% or greater increase in EPS of a company's stock over the last 3 to 4 quarters.

Relative Strength (RS) is a widely used indicator that measures the stock's price against past performance. The values range from 0-100. A value of >80 indicates that a stock is overbought. A value of < 20 indicates that a stock is oversold (possibly a buy opportunity).

Sales—is how much product or services a company has sold. You would like to see at least at least a 20% increase in sales over the past 3to 4 quarters.

Profit Margin—measures how much out of every dollar of sales a company actually keeps in earnings. You want to see at least a 15% or higher profit margin.

Return on Equity measures a company's profitability by showing how much profit a company generates with the money share holders have invested. When doing your research, you want to see at least 20% in return on equity.

Current Earnings are the earnings most recently reported by a corporation, which exclude tax and interest. Once again you want to see at least a 20% increase over the last 3 to 4 quarters.

Annual Earnings are the yearly earnings reported by a corporation which exclude tax and interest. Again you want to see at least a 20% or greater increase over the past three years.

Technical Analysis

What is technical analysis? Technical analysis is the charting of stock trading information used to predict the future trading action of any particular stock. Technical analysis is almost completely visual. An investor needs to know how to recognize and understand a charts action or direction. We will begin with the basics; charts, patterns, Indicators and trends.

Chart

- Candle sticks charts, line charts and mountain charts are used to view a stocks trading range. It tells you how much the stock is or has traded for in the past. The line chart (represented as a zig zag line on the chart) gives a general idea of the trading range for a particular stock. The mountain chart (which looks like a figure of a mountain on the chart) also gives you very limited information about the trading range. Unfortunately neither of the give you enough information about the stock's daily activity.

My personal preference is the candle stick. The candle stick tells you exactly how much the stock is trading for on any given day or week. The candle stick has three parts, the wick, the body and the tail. **The wick** –(which is the stem at the top of the candle) tells you how high the stock has moved that day: **The body –**(or the middle) tells you the price the stock opened that day (bottom) and how much the stock closed that day(top). The body is reversed when the stock has declined for the day.

The tail – the tail tells you how low the stock moved on that day.

The more information that you have about a stocks movement the better prepared you are to make a decision about future movement.

Below is an example of a candle stick in relations to stock charts. You may see different colors than the ones shown here. Black or green typically represent up days or weeks and red or gray typically represent down days or weeks.

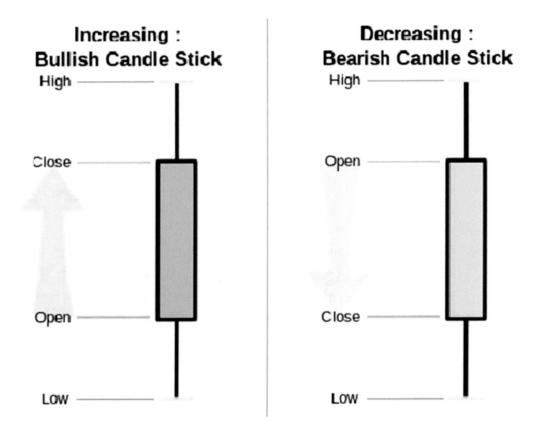

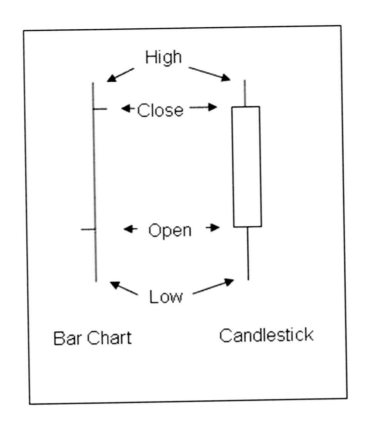

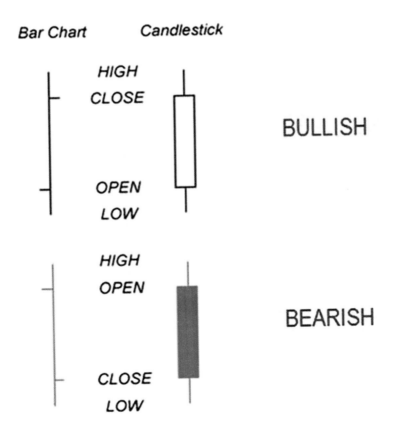

Chart Patterns

When looking at patterns, make sure that you are looking at weeks and not days. Patterns are typically measured in weeks. You can accomplish this by switching your charts over to 1 year or year to date on most chart software. There are many charting software to choose from. There are also some free ones that offer enough information to get you started. I am not promoting any software but I have found that MSN (money quotes) on the web to be very useful and it's free. I have listed below a few of the more common patterns to show you what to look for.

- **Double Top Pattern – M** (aka murder) this is a **sell signal**. This pattern is formed when a stock price climbs to a resistance level, bounces off and climbs right back to the same level of resistance. This is considered a reversal pattern.

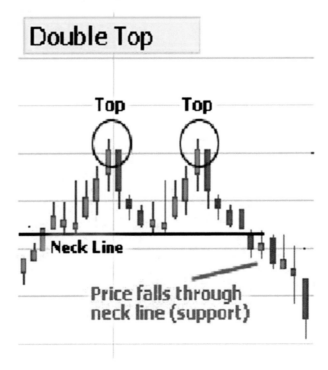

- **Double Bottom Pattern – W** (aka winner) this is a **buy signal**. This pattern is formed when a stock price falls to a support level, bounces off and falls right back to the same level of support. This is also considered a reversal pattern. The ideal time buy point is .20 higher than the middle of the W.

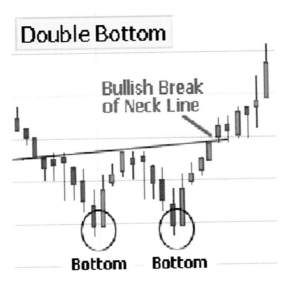

- **Cup and handle**—looks just like it is described. It has the shape of a cup with a handle. It is an ideal pattern for a potential breakout of a stock. **This is a buy signal.** The ideal buy point is .20 higher than the highest point of the handle.

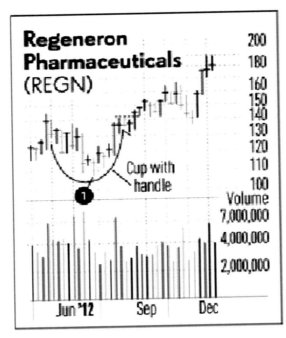

- **The three week tight pattern**—is described as a chart with tight closes for at least 3 weeks. **This is a buy signal**.

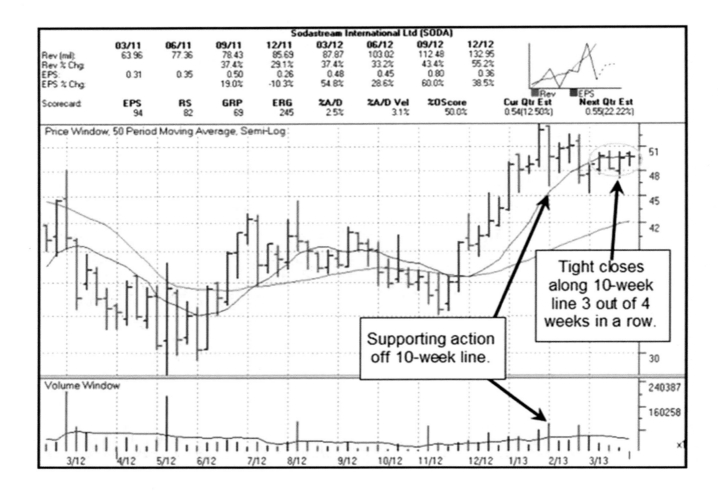

- **The golden cross**—is when the 50 week moving average crosses over and above the 200 week moving average indicating the upward movement of a stock. **This is a buy signal**.

- **The death cross** – is when the 50 week moving average crosses over and below the 200 week moving average indication the downward movement of a stock. **This is a sell signal**.

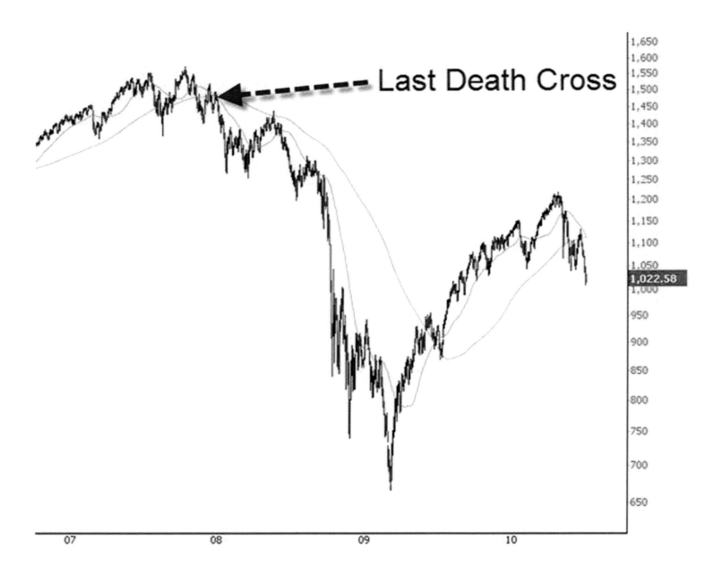

Last Death Cross

- **The flat base** – this pattern generally moves sideways. The buy point is .20 above the high of the base.

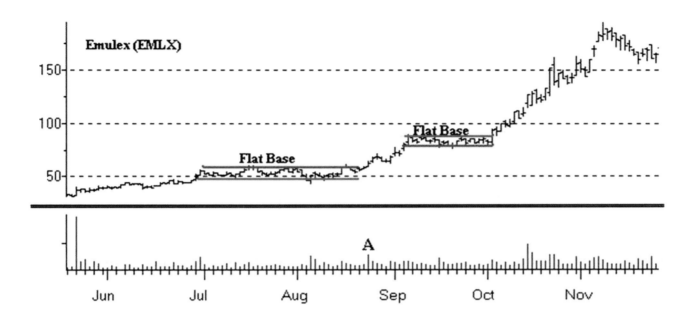

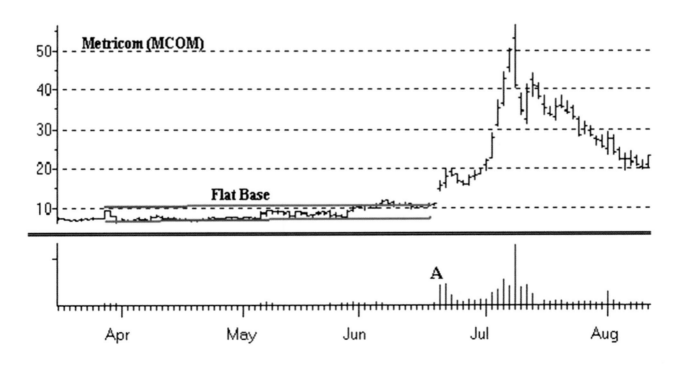

Support and resistance—support tells the investor how low a stock is likely to go and resistance will tell you how high a stock is likely to go. It will give the investor an idea of the trading range that that particular stock is trading in. The ideal time to buy a stock is when it bounces off the support line. I would also suggest that you be prepared to sell when it hits resistance.

Indicators

Moving averages (MA) – help you to identify a trend. It also serves as support or resistance depending on the trends direction. MAs show the past direction of a stock. They are generally separated into three time frames; short, medium and long. Short refers to short term. It is typically 10 or 20days of past activity of a stock. Medium is typically 50 days and long is typically 200 days of stock movement. Below we have simple moving averages 9, 18 and 36 day averages. I prefer the 10, 50 and the 200 day average.

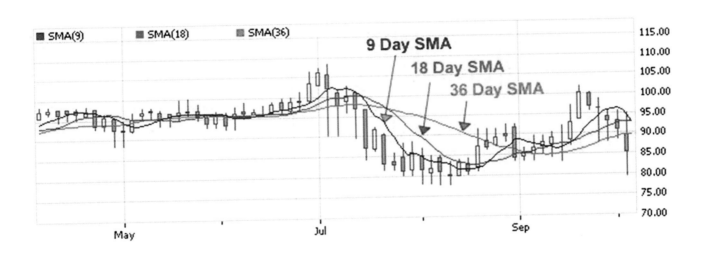

MACD – Is the moving average convergence divergence indicator which was created by Gerald Appel. It was designed to find up trends and down trends in a stock through its moving averages. It has three primary components. 1) Lagging indicator which tells what happen in the past. 2) Trending indicator which tells if the stock is trending up or downward. 3) Momentum indicator which tells the change in momentum.

MACD HISTOGRAM – The MACD Histogram was created by Thomas Aspray. It works on the same principles. However, it displays the moving average crossover in a different format (valleys and mountains). It has three functions as well. 1) It shows the moving average as it crosses over. 2) It measures the strength and momentum of the MACD. 3) It displays divergences. The red and blue lines are the MACD and the black lines are the MACD HISTOGRAM. **The buy signal** is when the MACD crosses up and over.

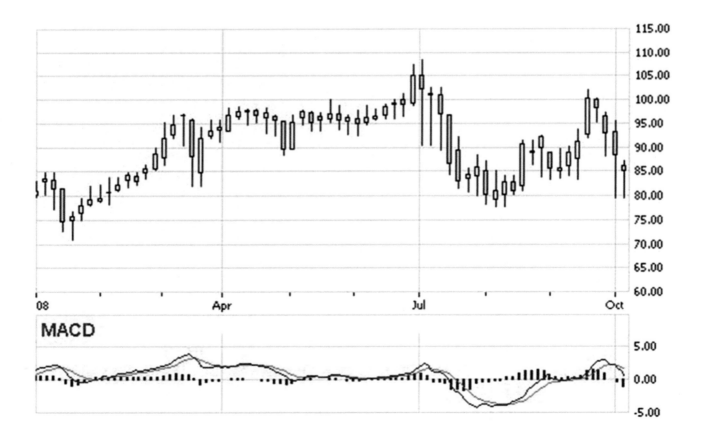

Relative strength indicator—Is a technique that compares the performance of a stock. It is the momentum behind the stock. Relative strength is used by many investors. It is a indicator that assumes a stock whose price has been rising will continue to rise. It can also be used to determine if a stock is over bought or over-sold. If the indicator is in the high range (60-90) the stock is considered over-bought. If the indicator is in the low range (20-30) the stock is considered over sold. Your best chance for success is finding stocks that are over-sold that meet all or most of your buying criteria.

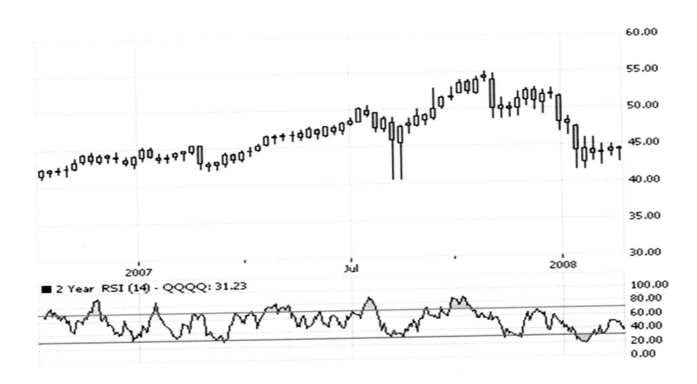

Stochastic – is a technical indicator which is used to determine the stocks up or downtrend pattern on a chart. The stochastic shows the oscillation of a stock when it is nearing or within an oversold area or an overbought area. The stochastic comes in two main varieties, fast and slow. They are both graphed between 0-100. Over 80 means overbought and less than 20 means oversold.

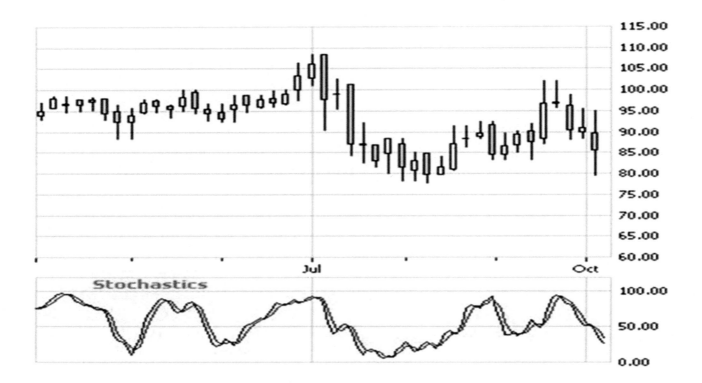

Accumulation and distribution—Is a momentum
indicator that attempts to gauge the supply and demand of a
stock. Accumulation indicates that investors are buying the stock.
Distribution indicates that investors are selling the stock. When
you decide to purchase a stock you want to see more weeks of
accumulation (blue) within the stock's pattern.

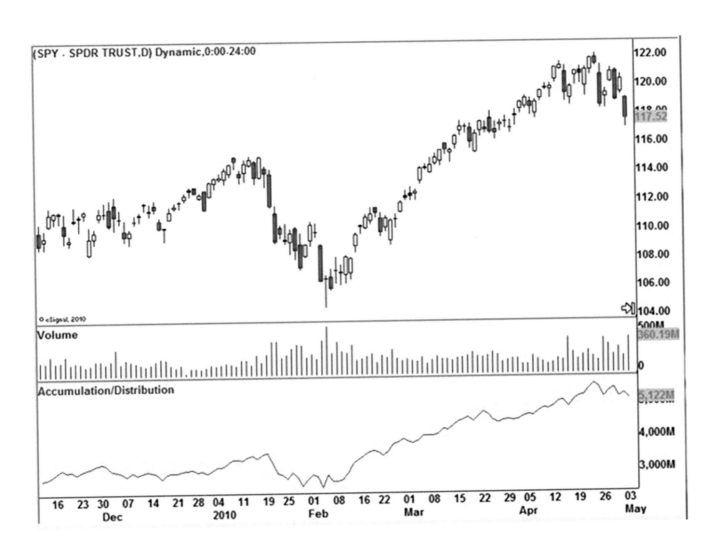

Trends

Uptrend—indicates that the overall market (or stock) is moving upward. When considering a stock purchase, make sure that overall market in an uptrend. You also want to see the stock that you are considering purchasing coming out of a proper base. Word for the wise, only buy when the overall market is in an uptrend.

Downtrend—indicates that the overall market or a particular stock is moving downward. Never buy when the market (or stock) is in a downtrend. There are advanced strategies to use in a downtrend (shorting stock) but for now we will stick to the basics.

Sideways trend (correction)—indicates that the overall market or a particular stock is trading sideways. When the overall market is moving sideways it could be an indication of a looming market correction. When examining a particular stock, it could be a sign of a flat base which is a buy signal. Always watch the overall market first before making a decision to buy. Remember the phrase that a trend is your friend. Never go against the trend. As before there are advanced strategies to play in a sideways trend (iron condor is a favorite for many investors), but for now stick to the basics.

Reading Stock Quotes

Reading stock quotes can appear confusing if you are new to the stock market. In this section, I will attempt to help you better understand the stock quote. Below is a copy of a Microsoft quote. On the top left you will notice the company's name and the ticker symbol used on the market.

Microsoft Corp. (MSFT)

Last Price	26.25	Last Trade	10/2/08	Tick	—	Volume	93.83 m
Change	▽ -0.23	% Change	-0.87%	Open	26.18	Prev Close	26.48
Day High	26.53	Day Low	25.70	52 Wk Hi	37.50	52 Wk Low	23.19
Bid	22.70	Bid Size	1000	EPS(TTM)	1.87	PE Ratio	14.20
Ask	27.50	AskSize	200	Shares	9.13 b	Market Cap	239.67 b
Dividend	0.52	Ex-Div Date	11/18/08	Yield	2.00	Exchange	NGS

Under the company's name you see the last price. **Last price** – this is nothing more than the last price that the stock traded for that day. Next you see change. **Change –** is the change in price of the stock for the day. In this case you can see that the stock was down (red arrow point down) .23 for the day. Underneath change you see the day high. The **Day's High –** shows you how high the stock traded for that day. In the middle of the page you will see open. **Open** – which tells you what price the stock opened on that day. The difference between the Day High and Open will give you a trading range for the day. This is an important factor for day traders.

Next you will see **52 week high** and across from that you will see **52 week low**. This tells you how high the stock has raised and how low it has gone in the past 52 weeks. This is an important factor when looking for trading range. I would also like to point out volume on the top right.

Volume – tells you how many shares were traded on the stock. You want to see a stock that trades at least 500,000 shares. Big money investors typically like to see a lot of volume or demand for a particular stock. On the bottom left you see dividend. **Dividend** – tells you how much the company is paying you for owning that particular stock (per share). It could be considered interest on you money or return on your investment. Most stocks pay dividends out to you on a quarterly base.

Risk and Reward Ratio

Risk and reward ratio—is the amount of risk that you are willing to take compared to the amount of reward that you will receive for taking that risk. Simply put it is the percentage of times that you received a reward compared to the number of times that you actually invested. Another way to look at is a risk/reward ratio of (3 to 1) states that I am willing to risk $3.00 to make $1.00 or risk 3 trades to make 1 successful trade.

The number one way to manage your risk is to use stop losses. Always determine your stop loss before placing your trade. In a good market I use a stop loss of 7%. In a bad market my stop loss is 5% of my purchase price. Successful traders know when to cut their losses and let the winning trades continue their run. Below is a formula for determining your risk verses your reward in your trade. B-buy price, T-target price, S—stops loss.

The stock's high	**H—7.55**	(for the previous day)
The stock's low	**L—7.32**	(for the previous day)
Your target price	**T—9.43**	(resistance or 25% of B price)
Your buy price	**B—7.65**	(.10 above the previous close)
Your stop loss	**S—7.12**	(-7% of your purchase price)
Possible gain	**Pg—1.78**	(difference btwn T & B price)
Risk	**R—0.53**	(difference btwn S & B price)
Reward	**R – 1.78**	(difference btwn B & T price)

Investment Strategies

We will now look at investment strategies. The strategy that you choose will determine how you will invest. You can either look to advisors or firms who will do most of the work for you (monitor the stock and give you buy and sell recommendations) or you can use the information that you have learned in this manual and do it yourself. FYI; the fastest way to lose money is to let someone else manage your money and the fastest way to gain money is to educate yourself and manage it yourself.

The first step is to exam the overall market (Dow Johns, NASDAQ, S&P 500). If the overall market is down, it is highly probable that the stock that you are interested in is trending down. It has been said that four out of five stocks will follow the market. With that being said, make sure that the market is in a confirmed uptrend before buying. There are strategies to play in a down market but those are advanced strategies such as option plays. For now we will stick to the basic. Only buy stocks when the overall market is in an uptrend.

Next, you need to do your research on any and every stock that you intend to buy. I discussed that in the previous section, Fundamental and Technical analysis. Remember, Fundamentals are the financials of a stock or company and Technical are the charts and trends of a stock.

Finally you will need to develop a set of trading rules or guidelines. Below is an example of some trading rules:

- Only trade in the direction of the trend-remember the trend is your friend.

- Only buy a stock after you have researched their financials and confirmed at least three buy signals—MACD crossing up, confirmed pattern (cup with handle, flat base, etc).

- Only buy at the predetermined entry point—.20 above the previous day's high or .20 above the high of the cup in a cup and handle pattern.

- Always use stop losses

- Never risk more than you can afford to loss.

- Never add to a losing trade.

- Go through the reward and risk ratio

- Always check for any news on the company especially the date of the next earnings report—which could change the direction of your stock depending on the report. Give yourself time to make money on the stock before that report comes out.

- Know your target—at least x25% of the purchase price or resistance on the chart.

Order Types

Order type is the communication or order that you give your broker regarding a trade or execution of a trade. Below I have listed some of the more common or basic order entries.

- **Limit order** – allow you to specify the price that you want for a stock. It basically says that you do not want the stock at the market price.

- **Market order** – is used to execute an order to buy a stock at the next available price. Unfortunately with this order type you cannot control what that price will be.

- **Stop order**– this order allows you to specify the price that you want. With a buy order, you would place your stop order above the market price (remember .20 above the previous day' high).

- **Stop Limit orders** – it combines the limit order with the stop loss. This order is used to place a trade at a specific price or better price.

- **Trailing Stop** – is considered a fancy stop loss. It adjusts the stop loss as the stock rises or falls in price.

Stop Loss

Stop Loss—is a strategy used to protect your investment. When used properly, it will limit your risk and contain your loses should the stock market change direction. A stop loss is a stop price (that you decide) you want your stock to be sold should things go south. Always, always use a stop loss when placing a trade.

A stop loss can be determined by either of two ways. It can be a set price that you decide or a percent of your entry price. Example; you purchase stock XYX for $18.25(per share). You may decide that you are only willing to risk $1.00 (per share) on the trade. Your stop loss would be placed at $17.25 (per share).

The other method with stop loses is using a percent of your purchase price. Again, you purchase stock XYX for $18.25 only this time you multiply the 18.25 x 7% = $1.27. You would then subtract the $18.25—$1.27=16.98 which would be your stop price. I personally prefer this method because it allows room for the stock to bounce before moving forward. Also, I typically use a stop loss of 7% in a good market and 5% in a bad market.

Remember, when a stock falls below your predetermined stop loss, sell the stock. Do not hesitate, ask no questions, no excuses necessary and no hoping that it will go up again. If the stock changes direction at a later date, you can always buy it again after you go through your buy check list.

Getting Started

Step one:

Find a broker. There are many stock brokers to choose from (Schwab, E-trade, Ameritrade, Fidelity, etc). I have no favorites. I personally decided to use an online broker. Reason being, online brokers allow me to have full control over my portfolio as well as the power to execute all trades. At this time I am using Tradeking and Optionhouse as my online brokers. I am not a salesman nor am I promoting either of the brokers. I chose these two because of the price that they charge to place a trade and their easy to understand trading software.

Step two:

Fund the account. This process will be determined by the broker of your choose. Some will allow wire transfers, some will allow back drafts and some will require that you mail them a check.

Step three:

Search for stocks to purchase. You can look at your local newspaper, trading journals, investor seminars or just simple word of mouth. I get my stocks from many sources. I go through about two hundred stocks a week looking for opportunities. I will be posting some suggestions on my web page for subscribed members www.hkinvesting.com

Step four:

Due your research. Always research your stocks before buying. Your research should include fundamentals analysis and technical analysis. Look for at 3 least confirmations of buy signals on both.

Step five:

Place your trade. After completing your research on the stock of your choice, place your trade.

Step six:

Place your stop loses on the trade. Remember you want to protect your investment.

Step seven:

Lock in your profits. As your stock moves up in price, increase your stop loss to lock in your profits.

Step eight:

Continue your education. Never stop learning. I have given you the basics to trading in the stock market. There is so much to learn, so many strategies for making money in the market. To become a successful investor, you will need to continue your education.

References

MACD (moving averages)—www.thehotpennystocks.com

The psychology of trading – www.esignal.com

Reading stock quotes – www.thehotpennystocks.com

Rich Dad Education – Fundamental and Technical Analysis

Stock chart pattern – www.amateur-investor.net

Stock chart pattern – www.marketwatch.com

Stock chart pattern – www.google.com

The Successful Investor by – William J. O'Neil

Picture 1

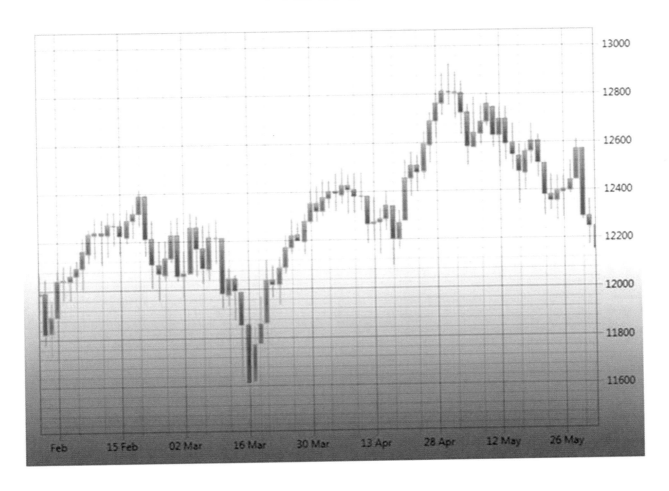

Picture 2

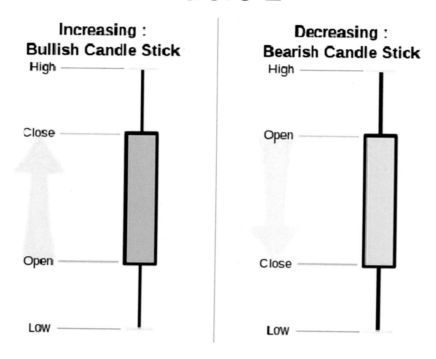

Increasing :
Bullish Candle Stick

High ——

Close ——

Open ——

Low ——

Decreasing :
Bearish Candle Stick

High ——

Open ——

Close ——

Low ——

Picture 3

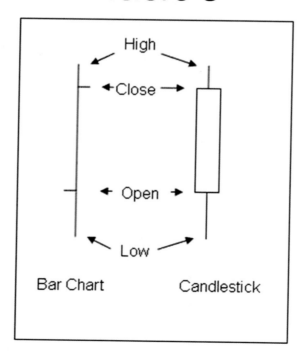

High

←Close→

← Open →

Low

Bar Chart   Candlestick

Picture 4

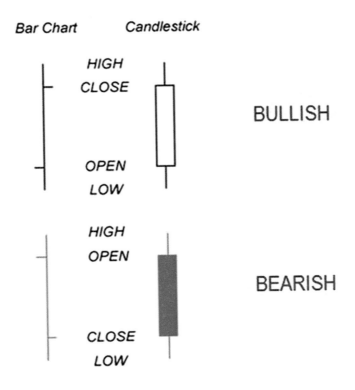

Picture 5

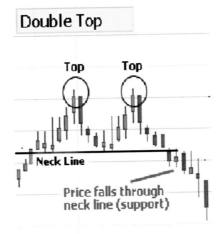

Picture 6

Picture 7

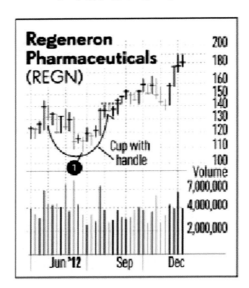

Picture 8

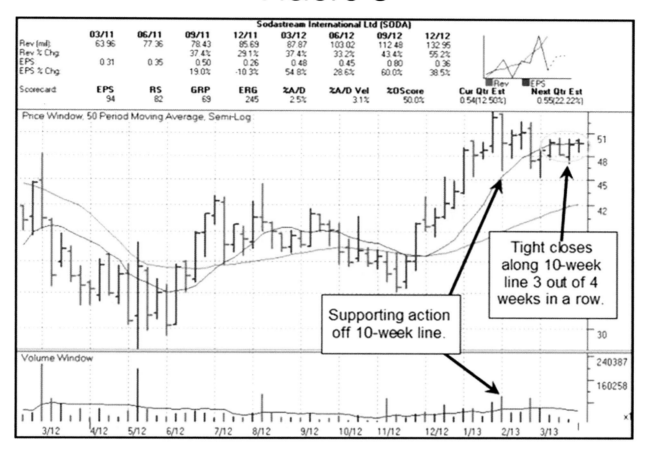

Picture 9

Picture 10

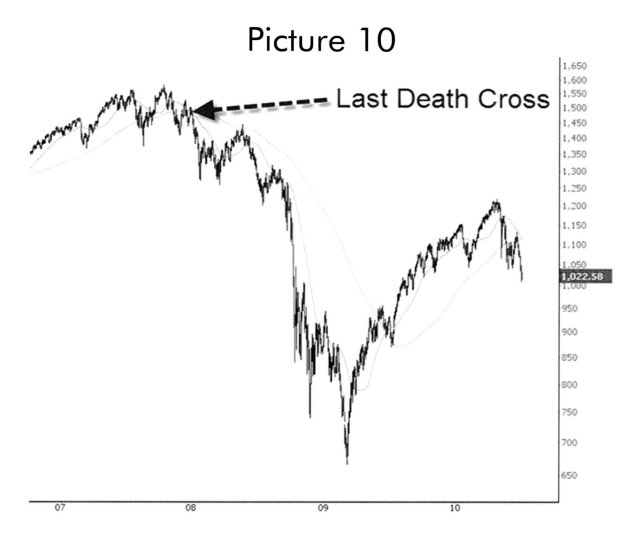

Picture 11

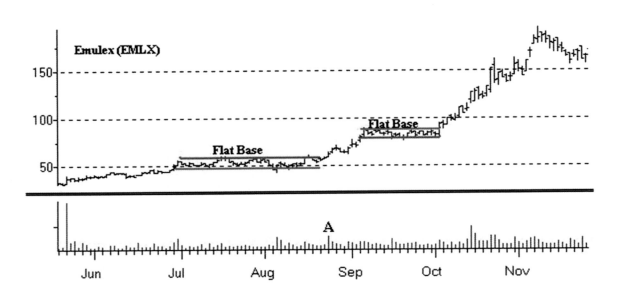

Picture 12

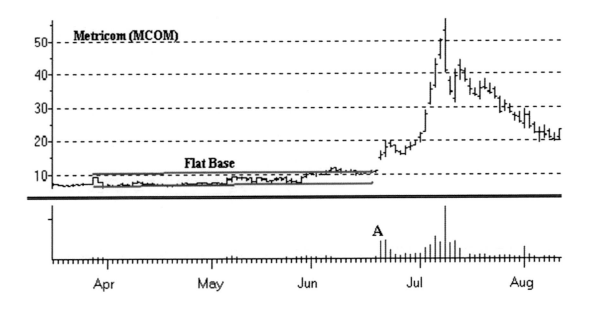

Picture 13

Picture 14

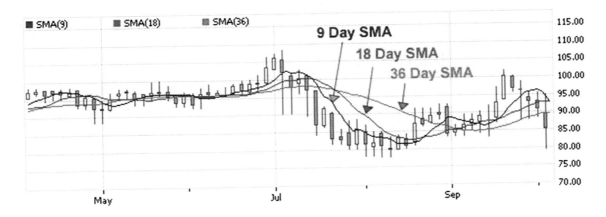

Picture 15

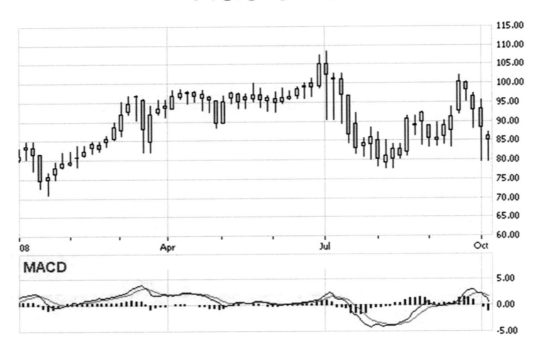

Picture 16

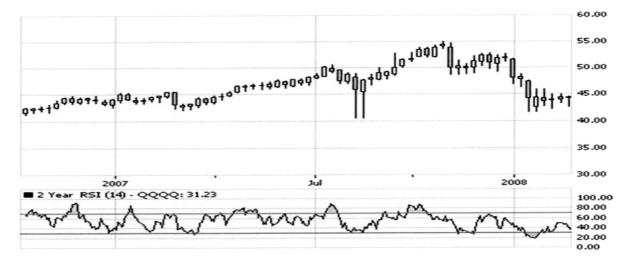

Picture 17

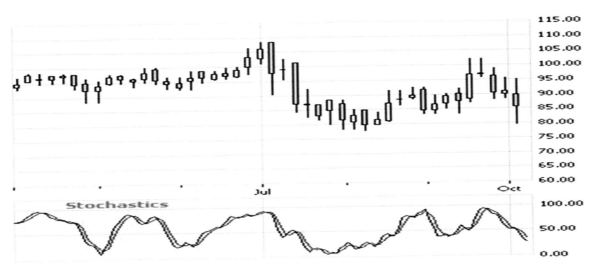

Picture 18

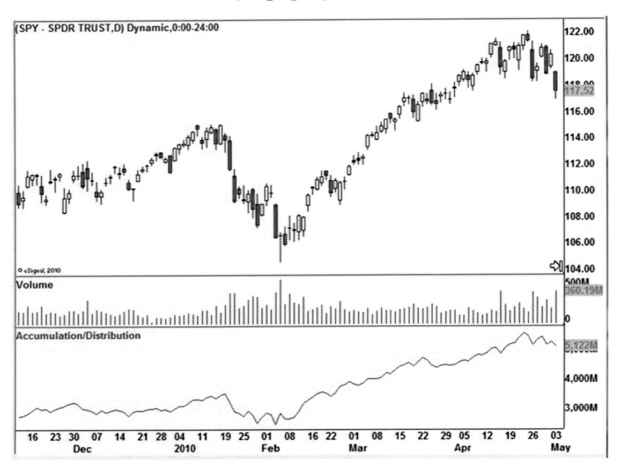

Picture 19

Microsoft Corp. (MSFT)

Last Price	26.25	Last Trade	10/2/08	Tick	—	Volume	93.83 m
Change	▽ -0.23	% Change	-0.87%	Open	26.18	Prev Close	26.48
Day High	26.53	Day Low	25.70	52 Wk Hi	37.50	52 Wk Low	23.19
Bid	22.70	Bid Size	1000	EPS(TTM)	1.87	PE Ratio	14.20
Ask	27.50	AskSize	200	Shares	9.13 b	Market Cap	239.67 b
Dividend	0.52	Ex-Div Date	11/18/08	Yield	2.00	Exchange	NGS

Printed in the United States
By Bookmasters